Usborne

Arts and Crafts
patterns
to
colour

Illustrated by Lise Herzog
Designed by Emily Beevers
Written by Hazel Maskell

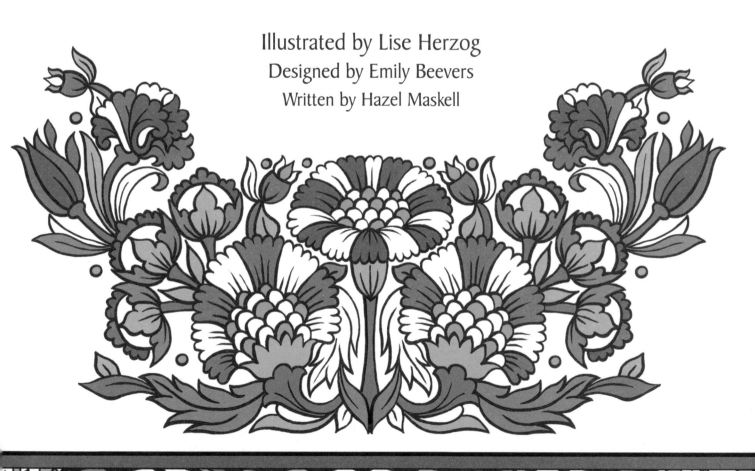

Arts and Crafts

Arts and Crafts was a style started in the late 19th century by a group of British artists, led by William Morris. It soon spread across Europe, America and Japan. Artists and designers believed that everything – from wallpaper to furniture and pottery – should be made by hand to the highest quality, and be beautifully designed.

Designs often included stylized animal and plant patterns. This pattern has birds among rambling roses.

Artists painted colours from nature – greens, browns and blues, and bright flowers or fruits.

Some artists looked to traditional Asian art for inspiration. This pattern has Japanese Koi carp and blue and purple peonies, a flower popular in China.

Traditional crafts

Arts and Crafts artists believed that everything should be made using traditional methods where possible. They hated the mass-produced, factory-made furniture and pottery that became popular during the 19th century.

This block of wood has been carved with a design. It can be dipped in paint or ink, and then printed onto paper or material.

Woodblocks were used to make wallpaper prints.

Plates and vases were often formed by hand, then painted by an artist.

Everyday objects

Entire houses were built in an Arts and Crafts style, and filled with furniture and accessories to match. Designers wanted their work to be useful as well as beautiful.

This chair has a simple shape, but striking patterns are carved onto its back and embroidered onto the seat.

Orchard tapestry

Hand-stitched tapestries were made to hang on the walls of Arts and Crafts houses. This design has an autumnal orchard with fruit-laden trees, intertwining branches and leaves, and wild animals.

Tapestries like this one were based on medieval designs from hundreds of years earlier. Use greens, blues, oranges and browns to fill in the scene.

Patterned pottery

Pottery was hand-decorated. Artists used patterns inspired by a wide range of different styles, from the Middle Ages to the Far East.

The pattern on this plate is influenced by medieval decoration.

An angel is standing in the middle of a vine of honeysuckle.

The thistle design on this vase is based on patterns from Turkey and Persia (now known as Iran). Colour the flowers blue and purple.

This vase is decorated with swans in an elegant style influenced by Japanese art.

On this vase, acorns are growing from highly stylized oak trees.

Wall decoration

Painted tiles or printed wallpaper added decoration to fireplaces and walls.
Some (on the left) were decorated with bold, bright patterns based on Persian and
Turkish art. Others, influenced by medieval art (on the right), were in softer colours.

Time for tea

Tea and coffee pots, cups, jugs and bowls were often made in an Arts and Crafts style. These designs are based on work by a group of American women artists at Newcomb College, Louisiana. They used yellows, blues and greens to create stylish patterns.

The teapot here has patterns made from the seed heads and leaves of iris flowers.

This is a sugar pot, decorated with pansies.

Colour these cups green, dark blue and yellow.

Use greens to fill in the leaves on this jug.

Colour the flowers on these bowls yellow, pale blue and cream.

The pattern on this coffee pot combines trees and pale pink flowers.

Fabulous fabrics

Arts and Crafts fabrics were often
coloured using natural plant dyes.
Many were decorated by hand,
by block-printing or embroidery.

Fabrics like the ones on this page would
have been used for furniture coverings.
Here they are shown on cushions.

Finish colouring these with dark blues, rich reds
and pale greens, blues and yellows.

Stained glass

Some designers created stained glass windows based on images found in old churches. The window below has women dressed in medieval-style clothing.

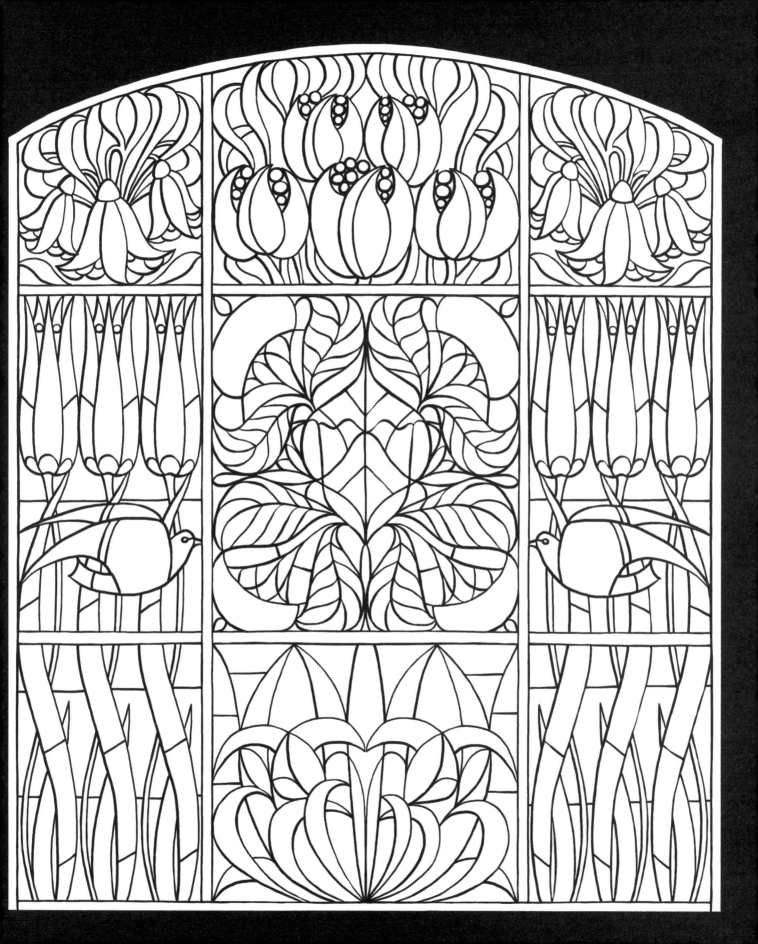

Arts and Crafts fashions

Fashion designers created loose, flowing dresses in rich colours, embroidered with patterns of flowers, leaves, and vines. Many based the shapes and decorations of their creations on medieval styles.

Flowers were popular natural accessories.

This robe is gold with white and pink flowers.

Colour this dress green and orange.

Dresses in these styles were famously sold at Liberty's,
a department store in London, which is still open today.

This robe has a turquoise
and pink vine pattern.

Colour this
Oriental-style coat
with gold.

Jewellery

Jewellery and other accessories were made of gold, silver or steel. They could be decorated with colourful stones, or with enamel – a type of bright glass fused to the metal.

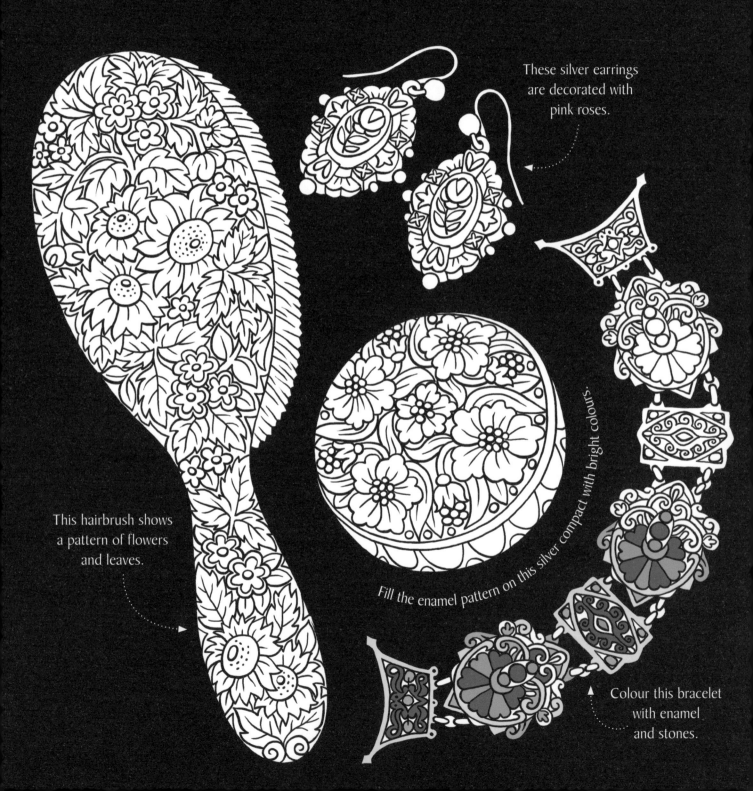

These silver earrings are decorated with pink roses.

This hairbrush shows a pattern of flowers and leaves.

Fill the enamel pattern on this silver compact with bright colours.

Colour this bracelet with enamel and stones.

This necklace is studded with diamonds, purple amethysts and pearls, surrounded by clusters of bright green enamel leaves.

This perfume bottle is engraved with a thistle pattern.

This is a silver hair comb. Colour the stones with light blues or pinks.

Books and printing

The most sumptuous Arts and Crafts books were bound with ornate leather covers that were dyed, then decorated with gold. The pages were printed with decorative type, influenced by medieval manuscripts.

Myths and folk art

This scene is based on hand-woven tapestries from Scandinavia,
inspired by myths, tales and traditional folk art,
as well as northern European landscapes.

The man on horseback in this scene is a famous 12th-century Norwegian king called King Sigurd. The robes of the dancing figures on the left are modelled on dragonflies. Use rich blues, greens and yellows for the figures, reds and oranges for the flowers, and a dark blue to colour the starry sky.

Arts and Crafts patterns

All the patterns on the following pages are based on designs found on
Arts and Crafts artefacts – prints, wallpapers, textiles, tiles and pottery.

Edited by Emily Bone. First published in 2015 by Usborne Publishing, Usborne House, 83-85 Saffron Hill, London EC1N 8RT, England. www.usborne.com

For links to websites where you can find out more about the Arts and Crafts movement and its key figures, including William Morris, Walter Crane, Charles Voysey and many more, and see examples of their work, go to the Usborne Quicklinks website at www.usborne.com/quicklinks and enter the keywords 'Arts and Crafts patterns'. Please follow the internet safety guidelines at the Usborne Quicklinks website. We recommend that children are supervised while using the internet.